JAZZ PLAY ALONG

Book and CD for B♭, E♭ and C Instruments

HAROLD ARLEN

10 Harold Arlen Classics

Arranged and Produced
by Mark Taylor

Photograph courtesy of S.A. Music Co.

For more information about the life and music of Harold Arlen,
Please visit the Official Harold Arlen Website at
www.haroldarlen.com

ISBN 978-0-634-06138-7

HAL•LEONARD®
CORPORATION

7777 W. BLUEMOUND RD. P.O. BOX 13819 MILWAUKEE, WI 53213

Visit Hal Leonard Online at
www.halleonard.com

Harold Arlen

Arranged and Produced by
Mark Taylor

Featured Players:

Graham Breedlove-Trumpet
John Desalme-Tenor Sax
Tony Nalker-Piano
Jim Roberts-Bass
Steve Fidyk-Drums

Recorded at Bias Studios, Springfield, Virginia
Bob Dawson, Engineer

HOW TO USE THE CD:

Each song has <u>two</u> tracks:

1) Split Track/Melody

Woodwind, Brass, Keyboard, and **Mallet Players** can use this track as a learning tool for melody, style and inflection.

Bass Players can learn and perform with this track – remove the recorded bass track by turning down the volume on the LEFT channel.

Keyboard and **Guitar Players** can learn and perform with this track – remove the recorded piano part by turning down the volume on the RIGHT channel.

2) Full Stereo Track

Soloists or **Groups** can learn and perform with this accompaniment track with the RHYTHM SECTION only.

AC-CENT-TCHU-ATE THE POSITIVE

CD
1 : SPLIT TRACK/MELODY
2 : FULL STEREO TRACK

C VERSION

LYRIC BY JOHNNY MERCER
MUSIC BY HAROLD ARLEN

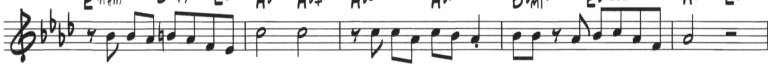

I'VE GOT THE WORLD ON A STRING

CD
3 : SPLIT TRACK/MELODY
4 : FULL STEREO TRACK

C VERSION

LYRIC BY TED KOEHLER
MUSIC BY HAROLD ARLEN

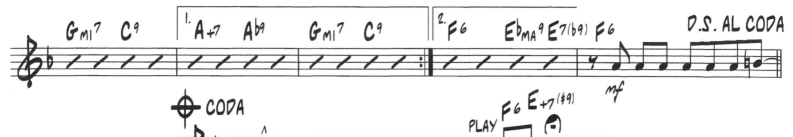

IT'S ONLY A PAPER MOON

LYRIC BY BILLY ROSE AND E.Y. HARBURG
MUSIC BY HAROLD ARLEN

CD
5 : SPLIT TRACK/MELODY
6 : FULL STEREO TRACK

C VERSION

IF I ONLY HAD A BRAIN

CD
◆7: SPLIT TRACK/MELODY
◆8: FULL STEREO TRACK

LYRIC BY E.Y. HARBURG
MUSIC BY HAROLD ARLEN

C VERSION

MY SHINING HOUR

LYRIC BY JOHNNY MERCER
MUSIC BY HAROLD ARLEN

C VERSION

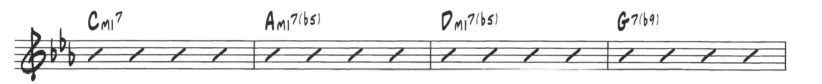

COME RAIN OR COME SHINE

WORDS BY JOHNNY MERCER
MUSIC BY HAROLD ARLEN

C VERSION

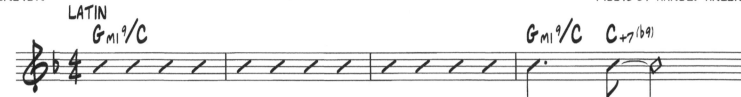

CD
⑬ : SPLIT TRACK/MELODY
⑭ : FULL STEREO TRACK

C VERSION

STORMY WEATHER
(KEEPS RAININ' ALL THE TIME)

LYRIC BY TED KOEHLER
MUSIC BY HAROLD ARLEN

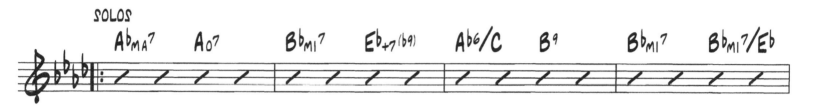

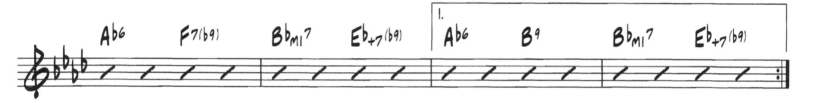

BETWEEN THE DEVIL AND THE DEEP BLUE SEA

LYRIC BY TED KOEHLER
MUSIC BY HAROLD ARLEN

C VERSION

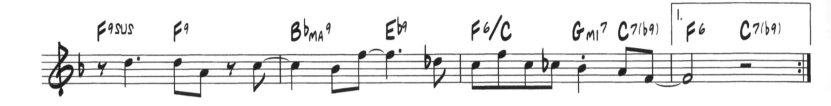

SOLOS (2 X'S)

| F6 | D7(b9) | Gmi9 | C9 | Ami7 | D7(b9) | Gmi9 | C9 | F9SUS | F9 |

| Bbma9 | Eb9 | F6/C | Gmi7 C7(b9) | 1. F6 | C7(b9) | 2. F6 | Bmi7(b5) E7(b9) |

| Ama7 | F#mi7 | Bmi7 | E9 | A/C# | Co7 | Bmi9 | E9 |

| C6/G | Ami7 | Dmi7 | G9 | Ab9 | G9 | C7(b9) |

| F6 | D7(b9) | Gmi9 | C9 | Ami7 | D7(b9) | Gmi9 | C9 |

D.C. AL CODA
LAST TIME
WITH REPEAT

| F9SUS | F9 | Bbma9 | Eb9 | F6/C Ab9 | Gmi7 C7(b9) F6 | Gb9 |

⊕ CODA

F6/C Ab9 Gmi7 C7(b9) F6/C Ab9 Gmi7 C7(b9) F6/C Ab9 Gmi7 Gb7(#9)

UNISON

OVER THE RAINBOW

LYRIC BY E.Y. HARBURG
MUSIC BY HAROLD ARLEN

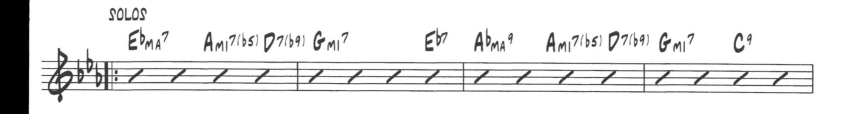

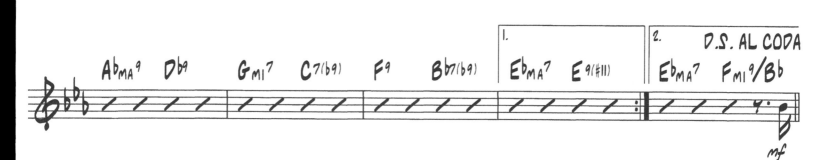

CD
19 : SPLIT TRACK/MELODY
20 : FULL STEREO TRACK

C VERSION

THAT OLD BLACK MAGIC
FROM THE PARAMOUNT PICTURE STAR SPANGLED RHYTHM

WORDS BY JOHNNY MERCER
MUSIC BY HAROLD ARLEN

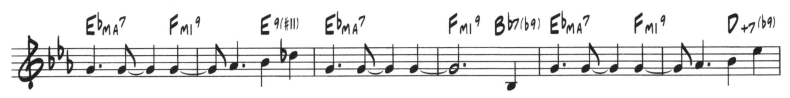

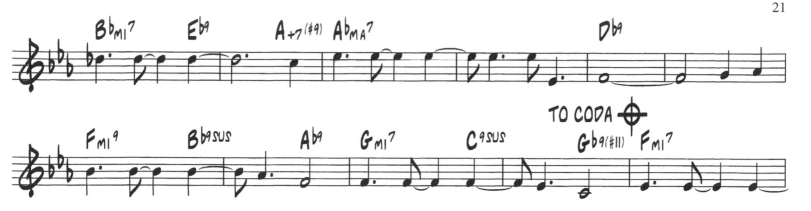

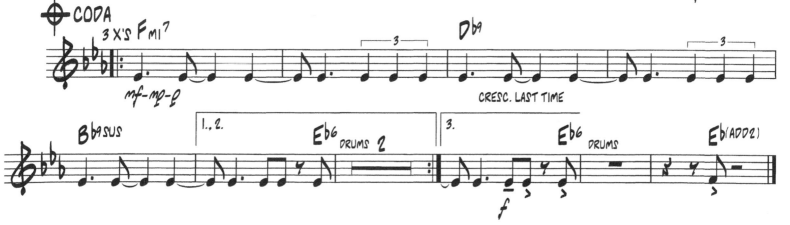

AC-CENT-TCHU-ATE THE POSITIVE

LYRIC BY JOHNNY MERCER
MUSIC BY HAROLD ARLEN

Bb VERSION

MEDIUM SWING

I'VE GOT THE WORLD ON A STRING

CD
3: SPLIT TRACK/MELODY
4: FULL STEREO TRACK

Bb VERSION

LYRIC BY TED KOEHLER
MUSIC BY HAROLD ARLEN

CD
5 : SPLIT TRACK/MELODY
6 : FULL STEREO TRACK

IT'S ONLY A PAPER MOON

LYRIC BY BILLY ROSE AND E.Y. HARBURG
MUSIC BY HAROLD ARLEN

Bb VERSION

IF I ONLY HAD A BRAIN

LYRIC BY E.Y. HARBURG
MUSIC BY HAROLD ARLEN

MY SHINING HOUR

CD
⑨ : SPLIT TRACK/MELODY
⑩ : FULL STEREO TRACK

B♭ VERSION

LYRIC BY JOHNNY MERCER
MUSIC BY HAROLD ARLEN

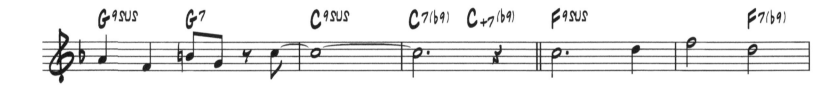

SOLOS (4 X'S)

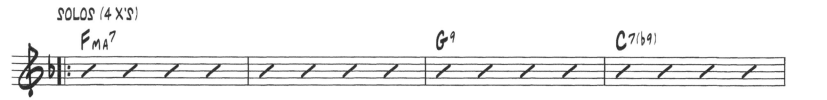

D.S. AL CODA
LAST TIME

CODA

COME RAIN OR COME SHINE

WORDS BY JOHNNY MERCER
MUSIC BY HAROLD ARLEN

Bb VERSION

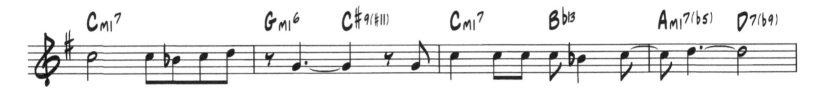

31

STORMY WEATHER
(KEEPS RAININ' ALL THE TIME)

LYRIC BY TED KOEHLER
MUSIC BY HAROLD ARLEN

Bb VERSION

33

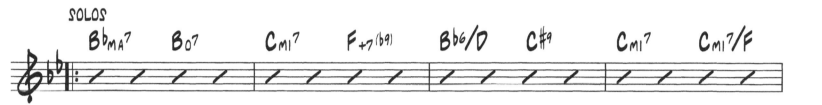

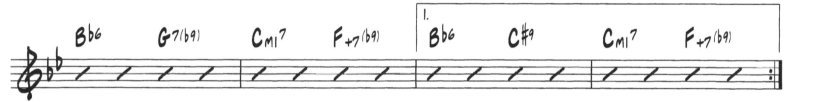

BETWEEN THE DEVIL AND THE DEEP BLUE SEA

LYRIC BY TED KOEHLER
MUSIC BY HAROLD ARLEN

B♭ VERSION

OVER THE RAINBOW

CD
17 : SPLIT TRACK/MELODY
18 : FULL STEREO TRACK

B♭ VERSION

LYRIC BY E.Y. HARBURG
MUSIC BY HAROLD ARLEN

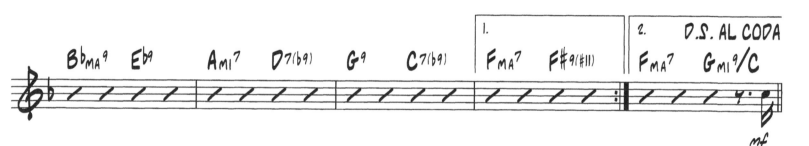

THAT OLD BLACK MAGIC
FROM THE PARAMOUNT PICTURE STAR SPANGLED RHYTHM

WORDS BY JOHNNY MERCER
MUSIC BY HAROLD ARLEN

B♭ VERSION

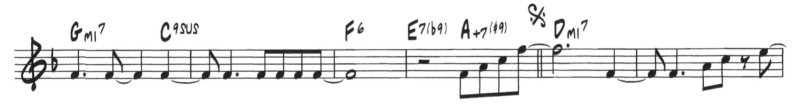

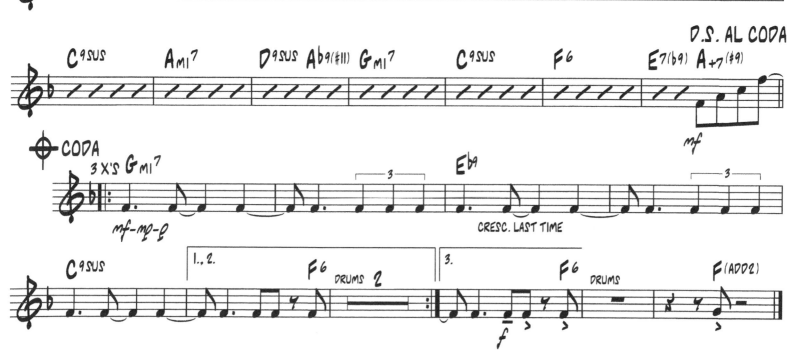

AC-CENT-TCHU-ATE THE POSITIVE

CD
◆1 : SPLIT TRACK/MELODY
◆2 : FULL STEREO TRACK

Eb VERSION

LYRIC BY JOHNNY MERCER
MUSIC BY HAROLD ARLEN

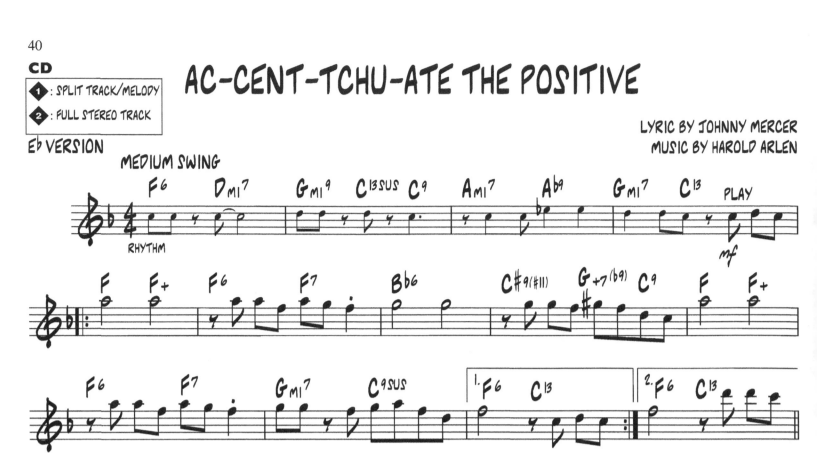

I'VE GOT THE WORLD ON A STRING

CD
③ : SPLIT TRACK/MELODY
④ : FULL STEREO TRACK

E♭ VERSION

LYRIC BY TED KOEHLER
MUSIC BY HAROLD ARLEN

CD
⑤ : SPLIT TRACK/MELODY
⑥ : FULL STEREO TRACK

IT'S ONLY A PAPER MOON

LYRIC BY BILLY ROSE AND E.Y. HARBURG
MUSIC BY HAROLD ARLEN

Eb VERSION

TO CODA ⊕

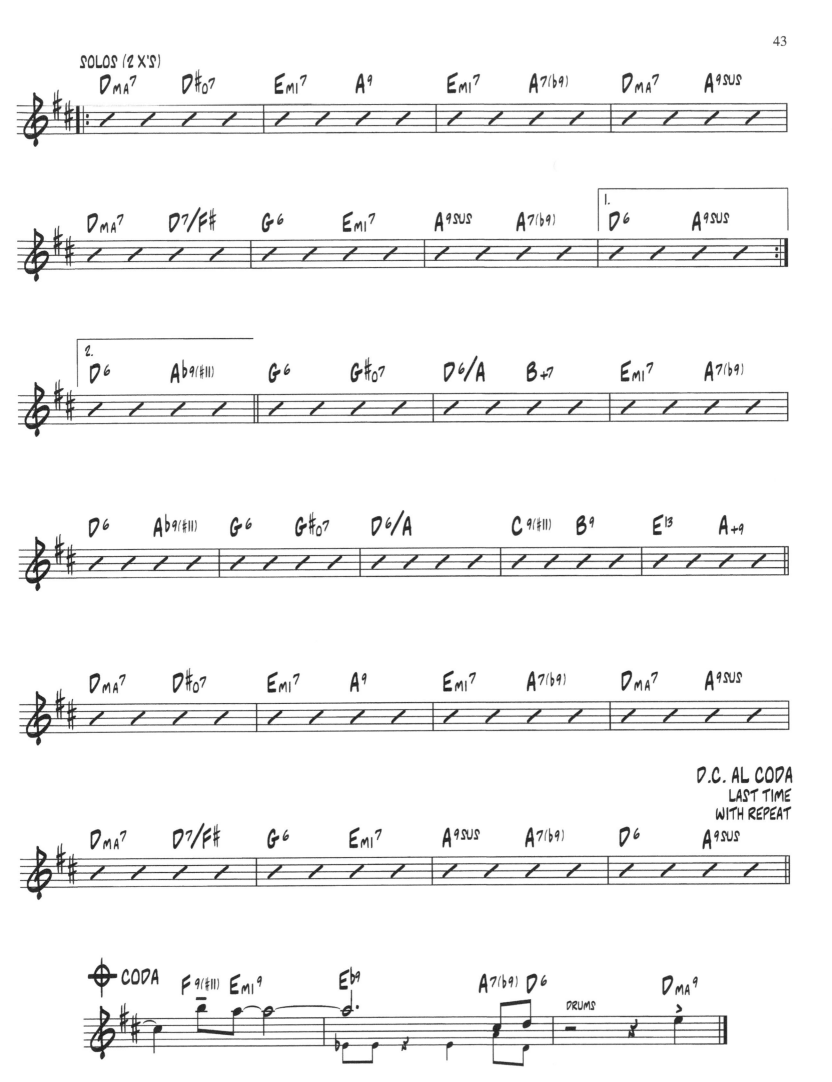

IF I ONLY HAD A BRAIN

CD
7 : SPLIT TRACK/MELODY
8 : FULL STEREO TRACK

Eb VERSION

LYRIC BY E.Y. HARBURG
MUSIC BY HAROLD ARLEN

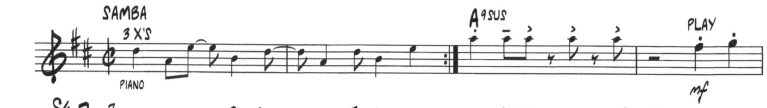

MY SHINING HOUR

CD
◆9: SPLIT TRACK/MELODY
◆10: FULL STEREO TRACK

Eb VERSION

LYRIC BY JOHNNY MERCER
MUSIC BY HAROLD ARLEN

SOLOS (4 X'S)

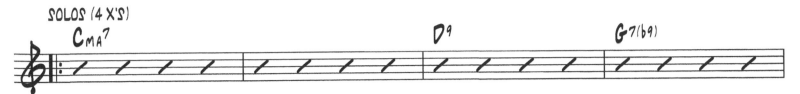

C MA7   D9   G7(b9)

C MA7   A MI7   D MI9   B MI7(b5)   E+7(b9)

A MI7   F#MI7(b5)   B MI7(b5)   E7(b9)

A MI7   D7   G9SUS   G7(b9)

C9SUS   C7(b9)   F MA9

E+7   Eb9SUS   D MI7   G7(b9)

C MA7   B+7(b9)   Bb9   A9SUS   A+7(#9)

D.S. AL CODA
LAST TIME

D MI9   G7(b9)   C6   D MI9   G7(b9)

CODA
C6   G#13(#11)   E13(#11)   C#MA13(#11)   C MA13(#11)

Come Rain or Come Shine

CD
◆11: SPLIT TRACK/MELODY
◆12: FULL STEREO TRACK

Eb VERSION

WORDS BY JOHNNY MERCER
MUSIC BY HAROLD ARLEN

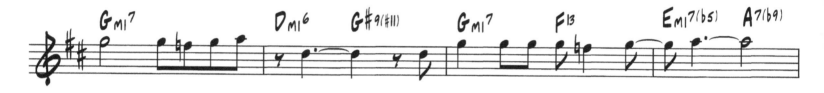

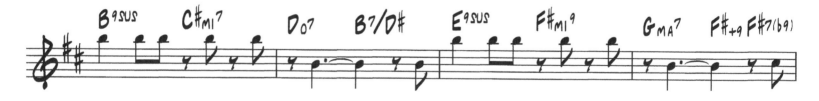

50

CD
13 : SPLIT TRACK/MELODY
14 : FULL STEREO TRACK

Eb VERSION

STORMY WEATHER
(KEEPS RAININ' ALL THE TIME)

LYRIC BY TED KOEHLER
MUSIC BY HAROLD ARLEN

51

BETWEEN THE DEVIL AND THE DEEP BLUE SEA

CD
- **15** : SPLIT TRACK/MELODY
- **16** : FULL STEREO TRACK

Eb VERSION

LYRIC BY TED KOEHLER
MUSIC BY HAROLD ARLEN

OVER THE RAINBOW

CD

17 : SPLIT TRACK/MELODY
18 : FULL STEREO TRACK

E♭ VERSION

LYRIC BY E.Y. HARBURG
MUSIC BY HAROLD ARLEN

SOFT LATIN

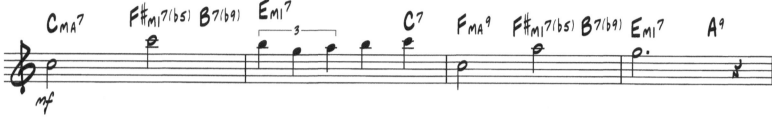

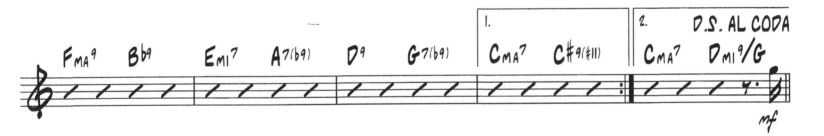

THAT OLD BLACK MAGIC

FROM THE PARAMOUNT PICTURE STAR SPANGLED RHYTHM

WORDS BY JOHNNY MERCER
MUSIC BY HAROLD ARLEN

Eb VERSION

CD
19: SPLIT TRACK/MELODY
20: FULL STEREO TRACK

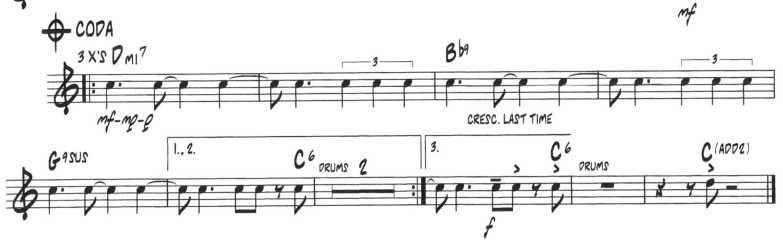

AC-CENT-TCHU-ATE THE POSITIVE

LYRIC BY JOHNNY MERCER
MUSIC BY HAROLD ARLEN

CD
: SPLIT TRACK/MELODY
: FULL STEREO TRACK

𝄢 C VERSION

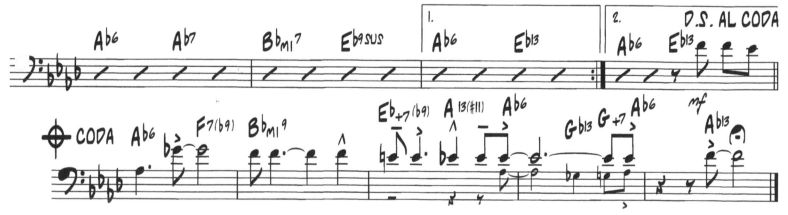

I'VE GOT THE WORLD ON A STRING

LYRIC BY TED KOEHLER
MUSIC BY HAROLD ARLEN

IT'S ONLY A PAPER MOON

LYRIC BY BILLY ROSE AND E.Y. HARBURG
MUSIC BY HAROLD ARLEN

CD
⑤ : SPLIT TRACK/MELODY
⑥ : FULL STEREO TRACK

𝄢 C VERSION

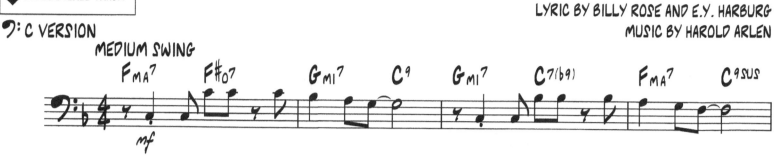

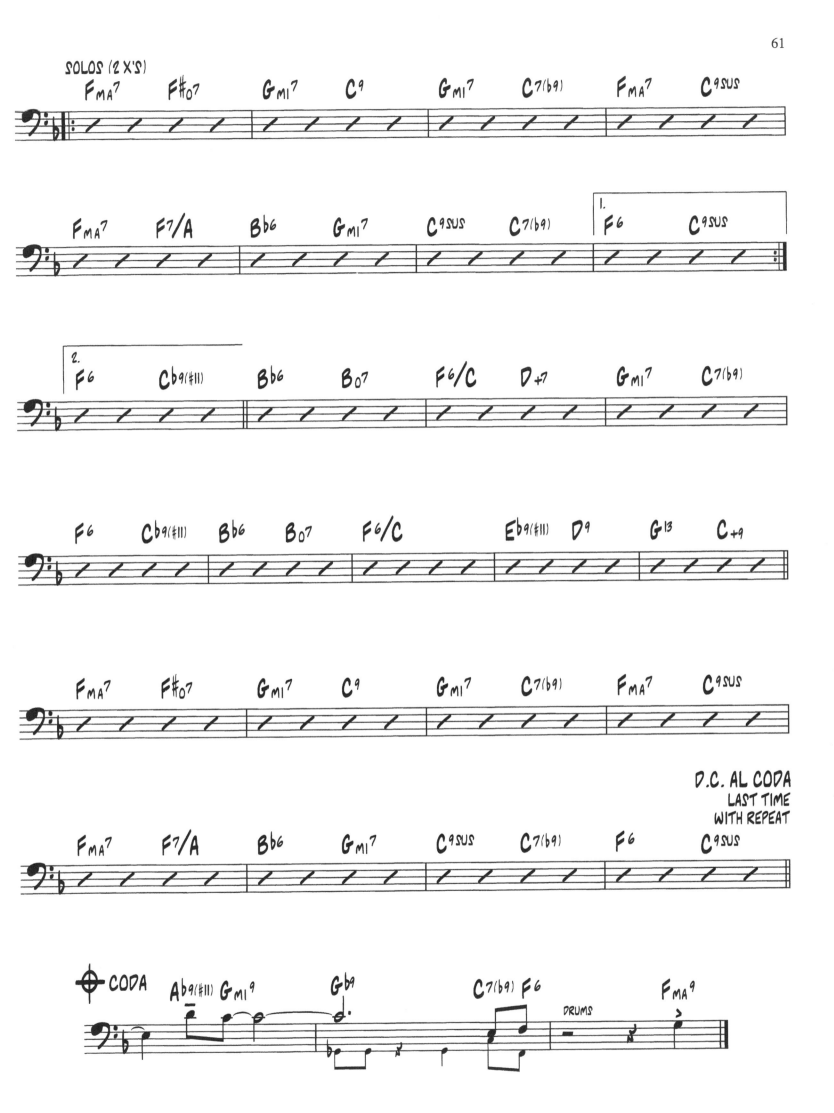

IF I ONLY HAD A BRAIN

LYRIC BY E.Y. HARBURG
MUSIC BY HAROLD ARLEN

𝄢 C VERSION

MY SHINING HOUR

LYRIC BY JOHNNY MERCER
MUSIC BY HAROLD ARLEN

CD
- 9 : SPLIT TRACK/MELODY
- 10 : FULL STEREO TRACK

𝄢: C VERSION

SOLOS (4 X'S)

E♭MA7   F9   B♭7(♭9)

E♭MA7   CMI7   FMI9   DMI7(♭5)   G+7(♭9)

CMI7   AMI7(♭5)   DMI7(♭5)   G7(♭9)

CMI7   F7   B♭9SUS   B♭7(♭9)

E♭9SUS   E♭7(♭9)   A♭MA9

G+7   G♭9SUS   FMI7   B♭7(♭9)

E♭MA7   D+7(♭9)   D♭9   C9SUS   C+7(♯9)

D.S. AL CODA
LAST TIME

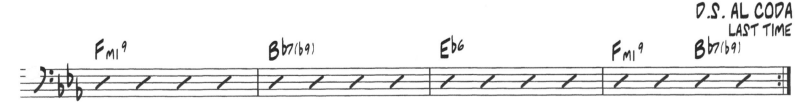

FMI9   B♭7(♭9)   E♭6   FMI9   B♭7(♭9)

⊕ CODA   E♭6   B13(♯11)   G13(♯11)   EMA13(♯11)   E♭MA13(♯11)

CD
11 : SPLIT TRACK/MELODY
12 : FULL STEREO TRACK

COME RAIN OR COME SHINE

WORDS BY JOHNNY MERCER
MUSIC BY HAROLD ARLEN

𝄢: C VERSION

CD

STORMY WEATHER
(KEEPS RAININ' ALL THE TIME)

LYRIC BY TED KOEHLER
MUSIC BY HAROLD ARLEN

𝄢: C VERSION

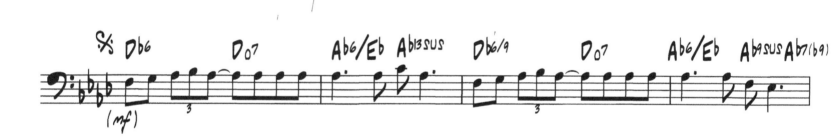

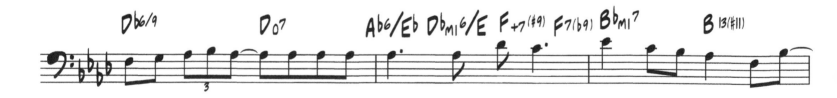

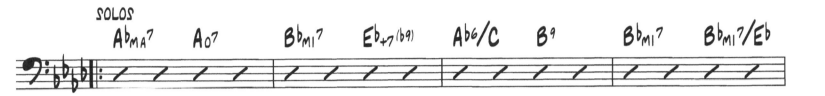

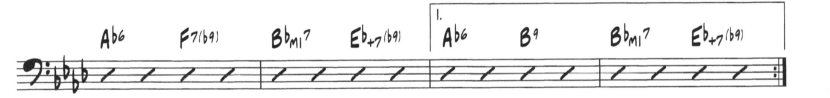

BETWEEN THE DEVIL AND THE DEEP BLUE SEA

LYRIC BY TED KOEHLER
MUSIC BY HAROLD ARLEN

OVER THE RAINBOW

LYRIC BY E.Y. HARBURG
MUSIC BY HAROLD ARLEN

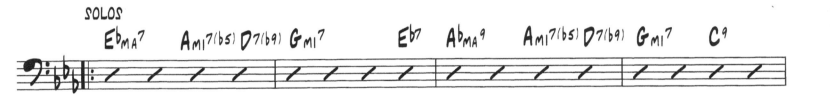

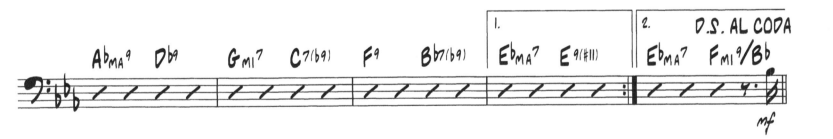

CD
19 : SPLIT TRACK/MELODY
20 : FULL STEREO TRACK

THAT OLD BLACK MAGIC
FROM THE PARAMOUNT PICTURE STAR SPANGLED RHYTHM

WORDS BY JOHNNY MERCER
MUSIC BY HAROLD ARLEN

C VERSION

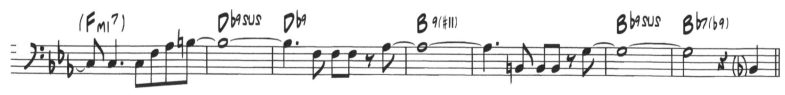

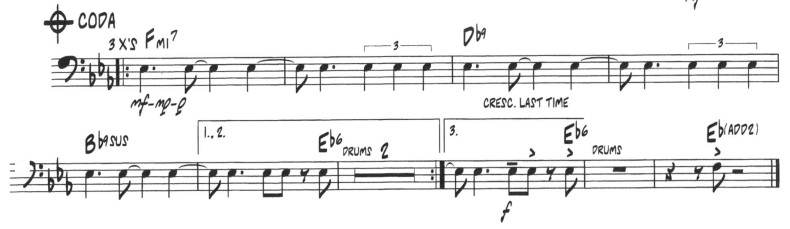

Lyrics

AC-CENT-TCHU-ATE THE POSITIVE

Gather 'round me,
Everybody,
Gather 'round me
While I preach some,
Feel a sermon comin' on me.
The topic will be sin
And that's what I'm "a-gin."
If you wanna hear my story
Then settle back and just sit tight
While I start reviewin'
The attitude of doin' right.

You've got to
Ac-cent-tchu-ate the positive,
E-lim-mi-nate the negative,
Latch on to the affirmative,
Don't mess with Mister In-between.
You've got to spread joy
Up to the maximum,
Bring gloom down to the minimum,
Have faith or pandemonium
Li'ble to walk upon the scene.
To illustrate my last remark
Jonah in the whale,
Noah in the Ark,
What did they do
Just when ev'rything looked so dark?
"Man," they said, "We better
Ac-cent-tchu-ate the positive,
E-lim-mi-nate the negative,
Latch on to the affirmative,
Don't mess with Mister In-between."
No! Don't mess with
Mister In-between.

BETWEEN THE DEVIL AND THE DEEP BLUE SEA

Is there anyone around who can not see
It's the well known run-a-round
You're giving me,
I suppose you'll tell me I'm all wrong,
It's a bitter pill to take,
Coming from you,
Tho' I've made a big mistake,
What can I do?
I don't know what makes me
String along.

I don't want you,
But I'd hate to lose you,
You've got me in between
The devil and the deep blue sea.
I forgive you,
'Cause I can't forget you,
You've got me in between
The devil and the deep blue sea.
I ought to cross you off my list,
But when you come knocking at
My door,
Fate seems to give my heart a twist,
And I come running back for more,
I should hate you,
But I guess I love you,
You've got me in between
The devil and the deep blue sea.

COME RAIN OR COME SHINE

I'm gonna love you
Like nobody's loved you,
Come rain or come shine.
High as the mountain
And deep as the river,
Come rain or come shine.

(continued)

COME RAIN OR COME SHINE
(continued)

I guess when you met me
It was just one of those things,
But don't ever bet me
'Cause I'm gonna be true if you let me.
You're gonna love me
Like nobody's loved me,
Come rain or come shine.
Happy together, unhappy together
And won't it be fine.
Days may be cloudy or sunny.
We're in or we're out of the money,
But I'm with you always
I'm with you rain or shine.

IT'S ONLY A PAPER MOON

I never feel a thing is real,
When I'm away from you.
Out of your embrace,
The world's a
Temporary parking place.
A bubble for a minute,
You smile,
The bubble has a rainbow in it.
Say, it's only a paper moon,
Sailing over a cardboard sea,
But it wouldn't be make believe,
If you believed in me.

Yes, it's only a canvas sky,
Hanging over a muslin tree,
But it wouldn't be make believe,
If you believed in me.
Without your love,
It's a honky-tonk parade,
Without your love,
It's a melody played
In a penny arcade.
It's a Barnum and Bailey world,
Just as phony as it can be,
But it wouldn't be make believe
If you believed in me.

I'VE GOT THE WORLD
ON A STRING

I've got the world on a string,
Sittin' on a rainbow,
Got the string around my finger,
What a world, what a life,
I'm in love!
I've got a song that I sing,
I cannot make the rain go,
Anytime I move my finger,
Lucky me, can't you see,
I'm in love?
Life is a beautiful thing,
As long as I hold the string,
I'd be a silly so and so,
If I should ever let go.
I've got the world on a string,
Sittin' on a rainbow,
Got the string around my finger,
What a world, what a life, I'm in love.

STORMY WEATHER
(Keeps Rainin' All The Time)

Don't know why
There's no sun up in the sky,
Stormy weather,
Since my man/gal and I ain't together,
Keeps rainin' all the time.
Life is bare,
Gloom and mis'ry ev'rywhere,
Stormy weather,
Just can't get my poor self together,
I'm weary all the time, the time,
So weary all the time.
When he/she went away
The blues walked in and met me.
If he/she stays away
Old rockin' chair will get me.
All I do is pray the Lord above
Will let me
Walk in the sun once more.
Can't go on, ev'rything I had is gone,
Stormy weather,
Since my man/gal and I ain't together,
Keeps rainin' all the time,
Keep rainin' all the time.

IF I ONLY HAD A BRAIN

Scarecrow:
I could while away the hours
Conferrin' with the flowers
Consultin' with the rain.
And my head, I'd be scratchin',
While my thoughts were busy hatchin'
If I only had a brain.
I'd unravel ev'ry riddle
For any individle
In trouble or in pain.
With the thoughts I'd be thinkin'
I could be another Lincoln,
If I only had a brain.
Oh, I could tell you why
The ocean's near the shore.
I could think of things
I never thunk before,
And then I'd sit and think some more.
I would not be just a nuffin'
My head all full of stuffin'
My heart all full of pain.
And perhaps I'd deserve you
And be even worth erv you
If I only had a brain.

Tin Woodman:
When a man's an empty kettle,
He should be on his mettle
And yet I'm torn apart.
Just because I'm presumin'
That I could be kinda human
If I only had a heart.
I'd be tender, I'd be gentle
And awful sentimental
Regarding love and art.
I'd be friends with the sparrows
And the boy that shoots the arrows
If I only had a heart.
Picture me a balcony
Above a voice sings low,

"Wherefore art thou, Romeo"
I hear a beat.
How sweet!
Just to register emotion,
"Jealousy," "Devotion"
And really feel the part.
I would stay young and chipper
And I'd lock it with a zipper
If I only had a heart.

Cowardly Lion:
Life is sad believe me missy
When you're born to be a sissy,
Without the vim and verve.
But I could change my habits,
Never more be scared of rabbits
If I only had the nerve.
I'm afraid there's no denyin'
I'm just a dandylion,
A fate I don't deserve.
But I could show my prowess,
Be a lion, not a mowess,
If I only had the nerve.
Oh, I'd be in my stride,
A king down to the core,
Oh I'd roar the way
I never roard before.
And then I'd rrrwoof,
And roar some more.
I would show the dinosaurus,
Who's king around the forres',
A king they better serve.
Why with my regal beezer
I could be another Caesar
If I only had the nerve.

MY SHINING HOUR

This moment, this minute
And each second in it,
Will leave a glow upon the sky,
And as time goes by,
It will never die.

This will be my shining hour,
Calm and happy and bright,
In my dreams, your face will flower,
Through the darkness of the night.
Like the lights of home before me,
Or an angel watching o'er me,
This will be my shining hour,
Till I'm with you again.

THAT OLD BLACK MAGIC

That old black magic has me in its spell.
That old black magic
That you weave so well.
Those icy fingers
Up and down my spine.
The same old witchcraft
When your eyes meet mine.
The same old tingle that I feel inside
And then that elevator starts its ride
And down and down I go,
'Round and 'round I go
Like a leaf that's caught in the tide.
I should stay away but what can I do
I hear your name and I'm aflame,
Aflame with such a burning desire
That only your kiss can put out the fire.
For you're the lover I have waited for.
The mate that fate had me created for
And every time your lips meet mine
Darling down and down I go,
'Round and 'round I go in a spin,
Loving the spin I'm in
Under that old black magic called love!

OVER THE RAINBOW

When all the world is a hopeless jumble
And the raindrops tumble all around,
Heaven opens a magic lane.
When all the clouds darken up
The skyway,
There's a rainbow highway to be found,
Leading from your window pane.
To a place behind the sun,
Just a step beyond the rain.

Somewhere over the rainbow
Way up high,
There's a land that I heard of
Once in a lullaby.
Somewhere over the rainbow
Skies are blue,
And the dreams that you dare to
Dream really do come true.
Someday I'll wish upon a star
And wake up where the clouds
Are far behind me,
Where troubles melt like lemon drops,
Away, above the chimney tops
That's where you'll find me.
Somewhere over the rainbow
Bluebirds fly,
Birds fly over the rainbow,
Why then, oh why can't I?

If happy little bluebirds fly
Beyond the rainbow,
Why oh why can't I?

THE REAL BOOK MULTI-TRACKS

TODAY'S BEST WAY TO PRACTICE JAZZ! Accurate, easy-to-read lead sheets and professional, customizable audio tracks accessed online for 10 songs

1. MAIDEN VOYAGE PLAY-ALONG

Autumn Leaves • Blue Bossa • Doxy • Footprints • Maiden Voyage • Now's the Time • On Green Dolphin Street • Satin Doll • Summertime • Tune Up.
00196616 Book with Online Media...........$17.99

2. MILES DAVIS PLAY-ALONG

Blue in Green • Boplicity (Be Bop Lives) • Four • Freddie Freeloader • Milestones • Nardis • Seven Steps to Heaven • So What • Solar • Walkin'.
00196798 Book with Online Media $17.99

3. ALL BLUES PLAY-ALONG

All Blues • Back at the Chicken Shack • Billie's Bounce (Bill's Bounce) • Birk's Works • Blues by Five • C-Jam Blues • Mr. P.C. • One for Daddy-O • Reunion Blues • Turnaround.
00196692 Book with Online Media $17.99

4. CHARLIE PARKER PLAY-ALONG

Anthropology • Blues for Alice • Confirmation • Donna Lee • K.C. Blues • Moose the Mooche • My Little Suede Shoes • Ornithology • Scrapple from the Apple • Yardbird Suite.
00196799 Book with Online Media $17.99

5. JAZZ FUNK PLAY-ALONG

Alligator Bogaloo • The Chicken • Cissy Strut • Cold Duck Time • Comin' Home Baby • Mercy, Mercy, Mercy • Put It Where You Want It • Sidewinder • Tom Cat • Watermelon Man.
00196728 Book with Online Media $17.99

6. SONNY ROLLINS PLAY-ALONG

Airegin • Blue Seven • Doxy • Duke of Iron • Oleo • Pent up House • St. Thomas • Sonnymoon for Two • Strode Rode • Tenor Madness.
00218264 Book with Online Media $17.99

7. THELONIOUS MONK PLAY-ALONG

Bemsha Swing • Blue Monk • Bright Mississippi • Green Chimneys • Monk's Dream • Reflections • Rhythm-a-ning • 'Round Midnight • Straight No Chaser • Ugly Beauty.
00232768 Book with Online Media $17.99

8. BEBOP ERA PLAY-ALONG

Au Privave • Boneology • Bouncing with Bud • Dexterity • Groovin' High • Half Nelson • In Walked Bud • Lady Bird • Move • Witches Pit.
00196728 Book with Online Media $17.99

9. CHRISTMAS CLASSICS PLAY-ALONG

Blue Christmas • Christmas Time Is Here • Frosty the Snow Man • Have Yourself a Merry Little Christmas • I'll Be Home for Christmas • My Favorite Things • Santa Claus Is Comin' to Town • Silver Bells • White Christmas • Winter Wonderland.
00236808 Book with Online Media $17.99

10. CHRISTMAS SONGS PLAY-ALONG

Away in a Manger • The First Noel • Go, Tell It on the Mountain • Hark! the Herald Angels Sing • Jingle Bells • Joy to the World • O Come, All Ye Faithful • O Holy Night • Up on the Housetop • We Wish You a Merry Christmas.
00236809 Book with Online Media $17.99

11. JOHN COLTRANE PLAY-ALONG

Blue Train (Blue Trane) • Central Park West • Cousin Mary • Giant Steps • Impressions • Lazy Bird • Moment's Notice • My Favorite Things • Naima (Niema) • Syeeda's Song Flute.
00275624 Book with Online Media $17.99

12. 1950S JAZZ PLAY-ALONG

Con Alma • Django • Doodlin' • In Your Own Sweet Way • Jeru • Jordu • Killer Joe • Lullaby of Birdland • Night Train • Waltz for Debby.
00275647 Book with Online Media $17.99

13. 1960S JAZZ PLAY-ALONG

Ceora • Dat Dere • Dolphin Dance • Equinox • Jeannine • Recorda Me • Stolen Moments • Tom Thumb • Up Jumped Spring • Windows.
00275651 Book with Online Media $17.99

14. 1970S JAZZ PLAY-ALONG

Birdland • Bolivia • Chameleon • 500 Miles High • Lucky Southern • Phase Dance • Red Baron • Red Clay • Spain • Sugar.
00275652 Book with Online Media $17.99

15. CHRISTMAS TUNES PLAY-ALONG

The Christmas Song (Chestnuts Roasting on an Open Fire) • Do You Hear What I Hear • Feliz Navidad • Here Comes Santa Claus (Right down Santa Claus Lane) • A Holly Jolly Christmas • Let It Snow! Let It Snow! Let It Snow! • The Little Drummer Boy • The Most Wonderful Time of the Year • Rudolph the Red-Nosed Reindeer • Sleigh Ride.
00278073 Book with Online Media $17.99

Prices, content and availability subject to change without notice.